Contents

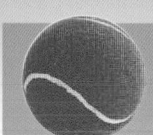# What is Tennis?

Tennis is an all-action game that requires great skill, speed, reactions and power. It can be played and enjoyed by men and women, young and old. Playing tennis regularly is a great way to help you get fit. At the top level, professional tennis players dazzle with their skills at sell-out venues all over the world.

Amelie Mauresmo of France powers down a serve on her way to beating Australia's Samantha Stosur at the Wimbledon Championships in 2006. Wimbledon is the only grand slam tournament (see page 7) to be played on grass.

How to Play

Tennis is played on a rectangular court by either two players in a singles match or two-a-side in a doubles match. Players stand on either side of a net, which is stretched across the middle of the court, and use a stringed racket to hit a ball back and forth over the net. They use a range of different shots from powerful smashes to delicate lobs or drop shots. The ball can only bounce on a player's side of the net once before it must be hit back. If a player fails to hit the ball over the net, hits the ball twice or hits a shot that lands outside the court, then the player's opponent wins the point.

Winning Millions

Amelie Mauresmo won the Australian Open and the Wimbledon Championships in 2006. These two grand slam events helped take her career match winnings to almost twelve million US dollars.

Games and Sets

A tennis match is divided up into sets of games. Some men's competitions insist on the best of five sets, others the best of three. To gain a set, a player has to win at least six games and be two games clear of his or her opponent. The tiebreaker system is used when a set is tied six games all. The first player to get to seven points or more and be two clear of their opponent wins the set.

Umpire and Rules

In tennis tournaments, matches are run by an umpire and officials including line judges. The line judges must spot whether the whole of the ball lands outside one of the lines. If it does, then the line judge calls the ball 'out'. If there is a dispute, the umpire has the final say. In casual games, the sport relies on players being fair and honest with each other.

Tennis Pros

There are thousands of tennis professionals or 'pros'. Most make their living teaching people to play the game. Only the very best compete on the major professional tennis tours for men and women.

Tennis players are expected to behave courteously towards their opponent, the umpires, officials and the crowd. Here, one player holds up the tennis balls which is a sign to her opponent that the tennis balls have been changed for new ones.

Agassi's Achievement

Andrei Agassi retired at the US Open in 2006, having played in more grand slam tournaments than any other man, 60 in all.

Grand Slam Events

The pinnacles of each season are the four major or 'grand slam' events – the Australian Open, the French Open, the Wimbledon Championships and the US Open. Winning a 'slam' competition is the aim of many pro players. For the very top players, winning all four slams is the ultimate aim. The last male player to do this all in one year was the great Australian, Rod Laver in 1969. Germany's Steffi Graf was the last woman to do it in 1988.

Tennis players are athletes. They must make quick decisions and move around the court fast. This player has used quick footwork to get into position to play a forehand drive shot.

Like many sports, tennis has a defined playing area, the court, and rules about how games are started and how points are won. Knowing the key rules will help you be a better player.

Tennis Courts

The surface of a tennis court varies and can be clay, grass, synthetic, cement hardcourt or artificial grass. Most courts in public parks are a type of hardcourt. Always treat a court well. Never leave litter, make holes in the surrounding fence or bounce or lean on the net. If it breaks, you will face injury as well as a large bill.

Game Scoring

Tennis has a unique scoring system. It can take as few as four points to win a game. These are scored as 15, 30, 40 and game. If a player has not scored a point in a game, his or her score is given as, "love". If both players win three points in a game, the score is 40-40, which is called deuce. To win the game from this position, a player has to win two points in a row. The first point is known as advantage. If the player with advantage wins the next point, it is game to them. If they lose the point, the score goes back to deuce.

Serving and Returning

Each game starts with one player serving the ball from behind the baseline and to the right of the small line on the baseline called the centre mark. They serve the ball overarm and aim so that the ball clears the net and lands in their opponent's service court diagonally opposite them. Serving the ball to win the point without the opponent touching it is called an ace. If the player's serve is out or hits the net and lands on their side, it is

The Court

Centre service line

Net

Net post

Left hand service court

Right hand service court

Service line

Doubles sideline

Singles sideline

Baseline

Centre mark

If the ball lands on the line it is in court.

Ball in

Ball out

If the ball lands outside the line it is out.

A tennis court measures 23.77m long by 8.23m wide for singles and 10.97m wide for doubles. The net stands 0.91m high at the centre service line but 1.07m where it is attached to the net posts.

This scoreboard at a Wimbledon Men's Singles semi-final shows that the score is 40-40 (deuce) in the sixth game of the fifth set. Three of the four previous sets went to a tie-break (7-6 or 6-7) in a match which Kevin Curran (pictured) eventually lost to Chris Lewis.

a fault and they are allowed a second serve. If that, too, is a fault, that makes a double fault and the point goes to the player receiving the serve. If the ball clips the net but lands inside the right service court, then an umpire would call first service (or second service if it is on the second attempt) and the server still has two serves. Once the point is won or lost, the server switches to the other side of the centre mark for their next serve and so on throughout the game.

Once the game has been won or lost, it becomes the other player's turn to serve a game.

Roger Federer is perfectly balanced as he guides a backhand volley over the net.

▼

Roger Federer

Date of Birth: August 8, 1981

Nationality: Swiss

Height: 1.86m

Weight: 85kg

Right Handed

Turned Pro: 1998

Tour titles: 45 singles, 7 doubles

Roger Federer is already considered one of the greatest players of all time. He has a highly accurate serve, responds well to the pressure to win key games and is comfortable in any position on the court. Following his first tournament win in 2001, Federer has gone on to appear in the finals of nine grand slams, winning eight of them. His one loss came at the 2006 French Open against Rafael Nadal. Federer's dominance of the Wimbledon Chapionships is extraordinary – including the 2006 tournament, he has won 48 matches in a row.

Ready to Play

You need to be sharp, fit and focused to play tennis well. Working on your shots and movement, getting advice and lessons from a coach and practising using drills and games are the ways to improve. Always seek out advice as you learn the game and take preparation before a match seriously.

Practice, Practice, Practice

Tennis relies on you being able to hit each type of shot well time and time again. The only way to achieve this is to practise long, hard and as often as possible. You also need a good eye and rapid footwork to get yourself into a good position to actually make the shot. A good tennis coach can not only point out mistakes in your technique or your footwork but can also suggest useful drills and fun games to play to improve your movement and your skills.

Warming Up and Stretching

Tennis uses a large range of muscle groups in your body, especially your back, shoulder, arm and leg muscles. Make sure that you fully warm up by jogging, running a few sharp sprints and performing star jumps. This helps get your body working and loosens up your muscles. Follow your warm-up with stretches to all your key muscle groups. Stretches prepare your muscles for the hard work ahead and help stop injuries. Perform stretches gently and carefully and ask others for advice if you're not sure.

Here are a small number of important stretches you should perform before playing or practising tennis. Ask your tennis coach or school games teacher for a full range of stretches.

Stretching

Keep both feet flat on the floor and ease down to stretch your calf muscle in your lower leg.

Stretch your side by bending across and down, running your hand past your knee.

Stretch your quadriceps (thigh) muscles by keeping straight and pulling your foot up to your bottom.

A baseball cap can reduce the glare from the sun.

This player is preparing to play with all the tennis kit she needs.

Long hair should be tied up so that it doesn't get in your eyes.

A sweatband helps remove sweat from the forehead in between points.

A loose-fitting and comfortable cotton sports top allows freedom of movement.

A tracksuit helps keep you warm before and after a match or practice.

Towelling socks help absorb sweat.

A water bottle – always take small sips of water or squash regularly during a match.

A small towel can dry hands and racket grip.

Some female players wear a ball clip to hold a spare ball.

This player is in a good ready position. Her knees are bent and her body is balanced so she can move in any direction. Her head is up with her eyes on the ball and both hands are on her racket which is also up, ready to move up or down or to either side.

Tennis Kit

Tennis clothing is often mainly white in colour and should be comfortable and loose to allow plenty of movement. If you wear shorts, ones with large pockets are good to hold a spare ball. The two most important items of kit are your racket and your footwear. Good tennis trainers should support your ankle, fit well and have a sole that grips the court. A good racket should feel comfortable in your hand and have the right-sized weight and hand grip for you. Get advice from a tennis coach before buying your kit.

Ready for Action

Make sure both your body and mind are totally prepared for a game. After stretching, start knocking up with your opponent. Knocking up is when the pair of players hit practice shots between each other. Take it seriously and concentrate on hitting the ball well and in the court. After hitting the ball, get into a good ready position to receive the ball. Give your opponent the chance to hit as well as you. It is all part of the spirit of the game.

The Forehand Drive

The forehand drive is likely to be the shot you play more than any other. It is known as a ground stroke as it is a shot mostly played after the ball has bounced once on your side of the court.

The Forehand Drive

The forehand drive relies on a long swing through the ball with the racket travelling from a low to high position. Footwork is important as you move from the front-on ready position to a side-on position with your front shoulder pointing towards your target. Don't try to hit the ball too hard. The key with the drive shot is a smooth, relaxed swing through the ball. If you time your shot well, this will generate plenty of power by itself.

The Forehand Drive

From the ready position, twist at your waist and turn your shoulders. Keeping relatively low, bring your racket back in good time before making the shot. Swing it forward with the handle end of your racket leading your swing. You do this by flexing your wrist back.

As you begin to swing the racket forward, step into the shot with the foot on the same side as your non-racket hand (which would be your left foot if you're right-handed). Keep watching the ball as it travels. Your arm should be almost fully extended as your racket connects with the ball.

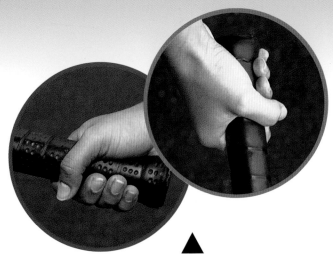

This is the Eastern forehand grip – a common grip used for the forehand drive. Grasp the racket as if you were shaking hands, wrapping your fingers and thumb around the handle and with your wrist behind the handle.

Practice Makes Perfect

Practise your forehand drive as often as you can with friends doing the same or up against a wall in a safe place. Don't worry if, at first, the ball often hits the net or sails out of the back of the court. Concentrate first on a relaxed swing through the ball from a low to high position. If you are still hitting the net, check your grip and that your racket is angled slightly upwards as you hit the ball. If the ball is flying really high, your racket may be angled upwards too much or you may not be stepping into the shot. As with all shots, a tennis coach can help you make the adjustments you need to improve your technique.

The Longest Career

Frenchman Jean Borotra has the longest career playing at Wimbledon. His last match was in the veteran men's doubles in 1977 but his first was in the singles competition in 1922, a span of 55 years.

Keep your eye on the ball and your body moving forward as the ball arrives. Aim to hit the ball when it is somewhere between knee and just above waist height. Aim also to hit the ball in front of your body and keep your wrist firm as ball and racket impact. The ball should fly away low over the net.

Let your racket arm continue to swing up and through after it has hit the ball. Your racket should end up pointing over your left shoulder. Move your back leg forwards and bend it to keep your balance. You can now quickly get back into the ready position, preparing for your next shot.

The Backhand Drive

The backhand drive is similar to the forehand drive but it is hit from the other side of the body. Mastering both forehand and backhand drives will give you the shots you need to play the ball back and forth in enjoyable rallies.

One-handed Backhand

Beginners sometimes make the mistake of staying front-on and hitting the ball with their racket in front of their body. Moving your feet early to get into a sideways-on position is essential. It allows you a full, free swing of your racket which is more likely to result in a strong, accurate shot.

The One-handed Backhand

● From the ready position, turn your shoulders so that your front shoulder points to your target. As you do so, use your non-racket hand to help you change your grip to a backhand grip (see page 15) as you swing the racket back.

● Support your racket with your spare hand as you swing back, bending your back low to help keep the swing low. As you swing forward, keep your eye on the ball and step into the shot so that more of your bodyweight is on your front foot.

● Make contact with the ball in front of your body. Keep your wrist really firm as you make impact, with the racket face angled slightly upwards. Your racket should follow through across your body in the direction that the ball is heading.

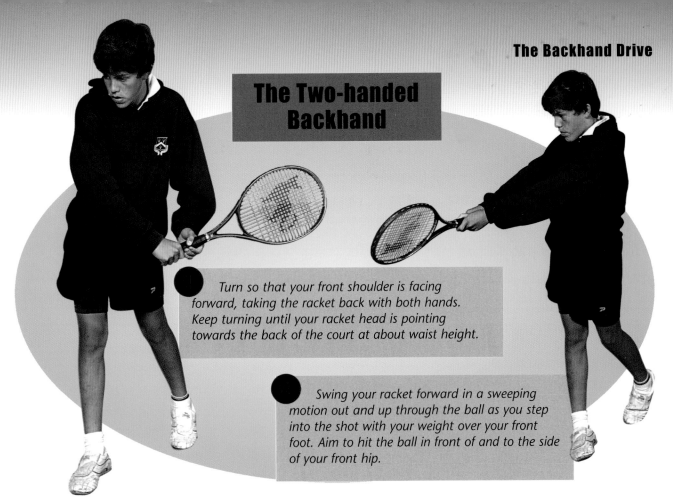

The Two-handed Backhand

Turn so that your front shoulder is facing forward, taking the racket back with both hands. Keep turning until your racket head is pointing towards the back of the court at about waist height.

Swing your racket forward in a sweeping motion out and up through the ball as you step into the shot with your weight over your front foot. Aim to hit the ball in front of and to the side of your front hip.

Two-handed Backhand

A player cannot reach quite as far for a ball with a two-handed backhand, but it does give players more support and control of the racket. It is a similar shot but unlike the one-handed backhand, the racket follows-through up and over, pointing high across your body or even over your shoulder.

Back and Forth

Practise both backhand drive shots with a friend gently lobbing balls to you. Once you are getting the hang of the shot, start practising on court with a partner. Don't worry about hitting the ball hard, just get used to the footwork, the swing and making good contact with the ball. Practise switching grip and moving from the ready position into the right position for both the backhand and the forehand drive shots. One of the best ways to do this is to practise hitting alternate forehand and backhand shots with a partner to gain practice in changing grips.

For a two-handed backhand grip, both hands should be wrapped around the racket handle. Ask your coach to help you with the two-handed grip and show you how to change to it from the ready position.

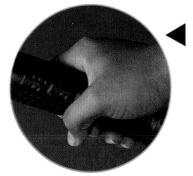

This is the a one-handed backhand grip used by many beginners. See how the inside of the thumb is held against the back of the grip.

Volleys

Volleys are shots that are played before the ball has bounced on your side of the court. They are mainly attacking strokes and mostly attempted when you are at the net or moving towards it. They are demanding shots to make but a good volley will often win you the point.

Fast Movement, Short Swing

Volleys are usually made when you are close to the net. This means you have less time to react to your opponent's shot, so you need to be fast and move into position as quickly as you can. The biggest difference between the volley and the drive shots is the length of the swing. Volleys are often hit with the minimum of racket swing back and with a very short, punched follow-through. It is important to hold your racket position and angle by keeping your wrist strong and firm when volleying, otherwise the ball may loop up into the air or out of control. The chopper grip (see page 21) is the best grip to use for volleying.

Forehand Mid-height Volley

The easiest volleys to make are mid-height volleys where you hit the ball between a little below waist height to a little below chest height. Get ready to volley by holding your racket up slightly higher and your elbows just in front of your body. Your feet should be spread shoulder width or slightly wider apart with your knees bent.

The Forehand Volley

From the volleying ready position, turn your shoulders to take the racket back a short distance, keeping it slightly above the height at which you aim to hit the ball and with the racket head angled slightly backwards. Keep your eye on the ball.

Turn your shoulders to bring the racket forward and lean forward into the shot. Aim to hit the ball in front of you with your wrist firm and very little follow-through. This will help punch the ball back.

High and Low

Volleys can come at all heights and angles. You need a really firm wrist for a high backhand volley so that the racket doesn't shake or twist in your hand as you make contact. Stretch up for the ball and try to hit it in front of your body, making sure your racket sends the ball across the net and down into the court. For a low backhand volley, you need to turn side-on quickly and get low by bending your front knee. This enables you to get the racket head underneath the ball with the face open (angled back) so that the racket carries the ball up high enough to clear the net.

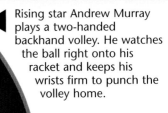

Rising star Andrew Murray plays a two-handed backhand volley. He watches the ball right onto his racket and keeps his wrists firm to punch the volley home.

Volley Practice

The volley is a relatively easy shot to practise. Use cones to make a 1-2m square in the corners of the court. Stand a little distance away from the net and ask a partner to hit balls to you at a height you can volley. Try to direct your volleys into the target square. After 10 to 20 shots, swap roles with your partner. You should also practise

your movement into the net to make a volley. Start just inside the baseline and, as your partner releases the ball to bounce it before making a shot, move in quickly towards the net. Your partner should hit the ball at a volleyable height. Aim to get into position to make the volley.

This player has just played a low forehand volley. She has bent her knees to get low and has leaned back just enough with an angled racket head to get the ball back over the net.

17

To get the best out of all your tennis shots, you need to be able to move quickly and smoothly around the whole court.

Watch and Move

Many failed tennis shots are due to the player being too close to the ball or having to stretch too far. The secret with hitting most tennis shots is to be in the right place before you have to make the shot. This allows you to be balanced and take the correct body and leg position into a tennis shot. Learning to read the flight of the tennis ball as it leaves your opponent's racket will allow you to move into the place where you predict the ball will arrive. This is comes with practice and with the experience of playing games. But quick feet

and movement can be worked on with a number of different drills.

Into Position

Sometimes, you will have to race to reach a ball that is angled wide or is close to the net. Getting the ball back into court is your first priority. Your next is to get back into a good position. This may mean you have to spring off one foot to get back into the middle of the court, back pedal (run backwards) to get further back or come forward to be close to the net. Coaches advise players to try to avoid getting caught in 'no man's land'. This is the half or mid-court area, around the service lines. In this position, you are usually too far away from the net to make a good volley and you may offer your opponent a good chance of passing you with a shot into the far corners of the court.

This diagram shows some of the types of shots you can play on a court. A cross-court shot (purple) is played diagonally and can catch out an opponent who is on the other side and unable to reach the ball in time. If your opponent is close to the net or to one side of the court, a shot down the line (blue) may pass them and result in a winner. An approach shot (red) may be used by a player approaching the net looking to make their next shot a winning volley.

A Really Long Rally

The longest known rally in a tournament occurred in 1984 between Vicky Nelson and Jean Hepner. The ball passed over the net a staggering 643 times before the point was won.

Hitting Winners

As you improve as a player, you will start to want to hit shots to win points rather than just to keep a rally alive. Hitting a winner is not all about power. Many beginners make this mistake and try to hit the ball too hard, but fail to keep it in the court.

Winning shots are more often about space and depth. A good, deep shot that drops just inside the baseline makes it harder for your opponent to return the ball. Look for space on the court that you can aim for, especially space that your opponent is moving away from. For example, if your

opponent has just had to return a ball from the sideline, they may start to rush back into the middle of the court. Hitting your shot back in the direction they are running away from may wrong-foot them and you may win the point.

Rafael Nadal

Date of Birth: June 3, 1986

Nationality: Spanish

Height: 1.85m

Weight 85kg

Left Handed

Turned Pro: 2001

Tour titles: 17 singles, 3 doubles

The first teenager to be world ranked number 2 since Boris Becker, Rafael Nadal began playing tennis as a four year old with his uncle, Toni Nadal, who remains his coach to this day. Considered the only player capable of taking on Roger Federer, Nadal is powerfully built, aggressive and lightning fast around the court. In 2006, he beat Federer in the final to win his second French Open title. Most famous as a player on clay courts who stayed close to the baseline, Nadal changed his game at Wimbledon in 2006 and came into the net a lot more. These tactics helped him reach the final.

Rafael Nadal chases down the ball in a match at Wimbledon. Always try to reach a ball and get it back in play. Your opponent may have relaxed and your surprise return may catch them out.

Learning to Serve

Serving starts each point of a game so it is a vital skill to master. A serve is essentially an overhead throwing action. Your target is to learn to serve accurately so that almost every serve lands in your opponent's service court.

Two Serves

Missing the service court, hitting the net and the ball bouncing back on your side of the court or hitting the ball twice during the serve all result in a fault. You are given a second chance when serving, but you should be aiming to get your first serve in. When practising and playing games at first,

The Serve

Start with the ball and racket at waist height or slightly higher together in front of you. The ball should be held lightly with your thumb and all four fingers, your knees should be slightly bent and your arms relaxed. Start to bring both arms down.

As the racket drops let it swing back with your arm close but the racket away from your body. Your arm holding the ball should start to rise as the racket swings back. Wait until your arm is straight before releasing the ball into the air. It should fly to your racket side and a little in front of your body.

Aim for the ball to peak at a height just above where you can reach with your racket. As the ball rises, your racket points upwards and is thrown over your head with your elbow kept high. Your weight should be over your front leg. Keep your eyes on the ball throughout.

just use one ball in your hand and wear a ball clip or shorts with deep pockets that can hold a spare ball. As you progress, you can get used to holding two balls in your hand when serving.

Ready to Serve

Start by standing around 50cm to the side of the centre line mark. You should be sideways-on with your feet shoulder width apart. Make sure your front foot stays behind the baseline. If it touches the line while you're serving, it is a foot fault which counts as a fault just like hitting the net or missing the service box. Beginners often use the forehand grip (see p.13) whilst more advanced players may use the chopper grip (see image on the right).

Serving Practice

Serving needs a lot of practice. Always take advice from coaches who can show you ways to practise the movements. Hit as many practice serves on a court as possible. You can also shadow serve, practising the basic swing and timing of your movements without a ball or court. Your ball toss is very important. You need it to be as reliable as possible. Top players can serve with their eyes closed as they know the actions of the serve really well and the height of their ball toss. You can practise your ball toss without a tennis court, holding your racket, adopting the correct stance and trying to send the ball to the right height every time.

The chopper grip is often used for serving. The V formed by your thumb and forefinger should be just to the left of the top of the grip.

Straighten your legs as you stretch with your racket arm to make contact with the ball. Aim to hit the ball just as it begins to fall with your racket arm straight. Follow through with the racket going across your body. Throughout the serve aim for smooth, flowing movements.

Your follow-through sees your racket ending up pointing behind you. Get your eyes on the ball and your body back into a balanced, ready position as quickly as possible.

Serving and Receiving

All players should work hard on their serve. It can be a major weapon in a match if a player's serving is good, and a major weakness if it is bad. The player returning serve has to be ready to pounce on weak serves and convert their chances into winning points in order to break their opponent's serve.

Serve Variations

Players need to develop pace and variety in their serves to outwit their opponent. The top players hit the ball fearsomely hard, but when starting out, aim for accuracy. As you improve and master your serve, you can begin to add a little more power and also try angling your serve so that the ball flies into the far corners of the service court. Good players watch where their opponents stand and are aware if they are weaker at playing backhand or forehand shots. Good serves send the ball deep into the corners of the service court, giving the receiver less time to get into position and react.

Receiving Serve

The player receiving serve must react to the serve, make good contact with the ball and get it back over the net and into play. From that point on, the ball is played back and forth over the net in a rally, with both players trying to seek an advantage and win the point. Players have to judge how hard and fast the server hits the ball and decide

Receiving Serve

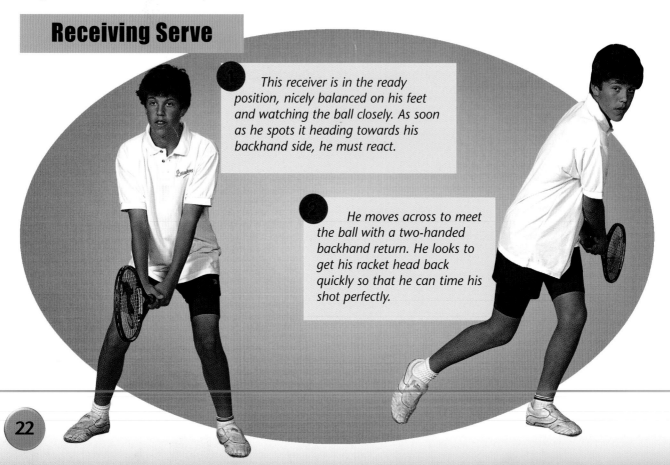

1 This receiver is in the ready position, nicely balanced on his feet and watching the ball closely. As soon as he spots it heading towards his backhand side, he must react.

2 He moves across to meet the ball with a two-handed backhand return. He looks to get his racket head back quickly so that he can time his shot perfectly.

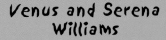

Venus and Serena
Williams

Dates of birth: June 17, 1980 (Venus)
September 26, 1981 (Serena);

Nationality: American

Heights: 1.85m (1.75m)

Weights: 72.5kg (66kg)

Both Right Handed

Turned Pro: 1994 (1995)

Tour titles: 11 (11) doubles, 27 (33) singles

Venus and Serena Williams grew up in a tough part of Los Angeles where they were coached by their father, Richard. The pair dominated women's tennis at the turn of the century with their incredibly powerful serving as well as strong ground strokes. Serena's first grand slam victory was the US Open in 1999. The day after she partnered Venus to win the doubles. Whilst highly successful in doubles as a pair, the sisters frequently appeared in singles finals against each other. Venus beat Serena to win the 2001 US Open but Serena won five grand slams in 2002 and 2003. Her opponent in each of these finals was her sister.

Serena (in the foreground) and Venus Williams are poised ready to receive serve.

whether to stand either outside, on or slightly inside the baseline. You should be in a position to cover serves which head both to your backhand and forehand side. As you improve, you can start to target your returns to winning parts of the court such as in at the server's feet or across the court so that the ball lands close to the baseline.

In a Spin

Serves and other shots can be played with spin which make them fly through the air differently and act differently after they bounce. Topspin is often added to serves and ground shots. This involves hitting over the back and top of the ball to make the ball spin forward so that it dips in its flight over the net and bounces up high after landing.

Slice is another common type of spin that sees a player hit across the back of a ball. This makes the ball curve to the left or right as it flies.

Speedy Serves

The fastest server in the women's game is Venus Williams who blasted a serve at 205km/h (127.4mph) at the 1998 European Indoor Championships in Switzerland.

Topspin sends the ball dipping down at the end of its flight.

Backspin sees the ball brake when it hits the ground.

Advanced Shots

There are many different shots in tennis. Many are variations on the forehand and backhand drive or are volleys made at different heights and angles. The smash, lob and drop shot are three advanced shots which are used in matches.

The Smash

This is an overhead shot mostly played on the forehand side which can be used to put away a high ball. The action is similar to that of a serve, with the racket thrown upwards and swinging down through the ball. Timing the smash so that the racket angle sends the ball down into your opponent's court is crucial. When working

on smashes, concentrate on the angle of your racket and the point at which it meets the ball. Rather than trying to thump the ball hard, concentrate on guiding the ball away from your opponent so that they cannot reach it to return it. The backhand smash is a very tricky shot to master. If the ball loops high in the air on your backhand side, you can sometimes move quickly across so that you can hit the ball on your forehand side.

The Lob

The lob shot is a looping shot usually designed to rise over and out of the reach of your opponent who is coming to or is at the net. A good lob shouldn't sail too high into the air as that may give your opponent time to recover. Lobs can be played on the backhand or forehand side. Your body position and movement for a forehand lob is very similar to the forehand drive. The key differences are that you swing

This player is practising her overhead smash. She aims to stretch her body to hit the ball ahead of her.

Four in a Row

Serena Williams was the last woman to win four grand slam tournaments in a row. She won three in 2002 and then the first slam of 2003, the Australian Open.

Backhand Lob

This player has put up a backhand lob which has cleared her opponent at the net. Try practising hitting lob and drive shots alternately to see the difference in the action and the movement of the ball.

the racket from a very low position to a high one and you keep the racket face open as you hit the ball to generate the lift. Experienced players add topspin (see page 23) to their lob shots. Using topspin helps the ball drop down more sharply and gives opponents less time to react.

Drop Shots

The drop shot is a gentle shot where the player takes the pace and power off the ball to send it travelling just over the net. A good drop shot adds backspin (see page 23) to the ball which means that when it bounces it will not bounce forward very far. This makes it harder for an opponent to play the ball. Against an opponent who is behind the baseline, a drop shot can often win a point or, at the very least, force an opponent out of position. Drop shots can be played on both backhand and forehand sides.

The key is to have a relaxed yet controlled grip, to slice or hit the back and bottom of the ball to add backspin and to make contact with the ball with the racket face angled back.

This player attempts a forehand drop shot. She leads with the bottom edge of her racket and aims to play the ball softly and delicately with her racket face angled back.

25

Playing Doubles

Doubles is a fast, fun and exciting alternative to playing singles matches. It may appear less energetic but this can be an illusion. The court is wider (see page 8) and the ball zips around often at a greater range of angles than in the singles game. Doubles calls for brilliant reactions and excellent teamwork between a pair of players.

Serving in Doubles

Serving in doubles is a little more complicated than in singles. In every four games, each player must serve a game and in the right order. The first serving pair usually let their best server go first. Their partner will serve third and their opponents will serve second and fourth. When serving, both players decide where the server's partner should stand. They might choose to stand quite close to the net in order to make a strong volley. If the server has a weak serve or is on a second serve, their partner may opt for a more defensive position and stand further back.

Returns and Rallies

The returning player notes where their opponents are positioned and will often try to hit a low, accurate shot over the net, and away from the opponent at the net. Once the ball has been served and returned, any player can play the ball providing each pair only strike the ball once. Each player in a pair takes responsibility for one side of the court. If a player crosses sides to make a shot, then the other player must move to cover their team-mate's side which is now open.

Tactics and Teamwork

Doubles might require less movement around the whole court on every point, but it still requires fast footwork and even faster reactions. Excellent volleying is important as many points are won or lost at the net. An expert volleyer can launch themself at the ball to intercept it. Rallies in doubles can be long and exciting. Always keep an eye out for space or an angle of shot which can result in a winning shot.

In doubles, players often serve roughly halfway between the centre service line and the sideline. This allows them to cover their side of the court once a rally begins. Here, their partner stands close to the net ready to pounce on a weak return and put away a volley.

Martina Navratilova

Date of Birth: October 18, 1956

Nationality: American

Height: 1.73m

Weight: 65kg

Left Handed

Turned Pro: 1975

Tour titles: 168 singles, 176 doubles

Born in Czechoslovakia (now the Czech Republic), Navratilova was the ultimate tennis competitor. She is thought of as the greatest female player of all time. Supremely fit and a brilliant volleyer at the net, she won an extraordinary 31 Grand Slam titles in ladies doubles. To this record tally can be added a further nine grand slam titles in mixed doubles and 18 grand slam singles titles. A legend to a new generation of players, Navratilova won her latest tour title in 2006, just short of her 50th birthday.

Players choose to cover sides of the court or one may cover the net and the other the back of the court. Here, a player has reached high to hit a tricky backhand overhead shot.

Martina Navratilova reaches for a backhand volley during a doubles match at Wimbledon.

In August 2006, two months shy of her 50th birthday, Martina Navratilova captured her 353rd tournament title, winning the women's doubles with Nadia Petrova at the Rogers Cup in Canada.

Records and Achievements

Most Grand Slam Singles Titles

Men
Pete Sampras 14
Roy Emerson 12
Rod Laver 11
Bjorn Borg 11
Bill Tilden 10

Women
Margaret Smith Court 24
Steffi Graf 22
Helen Wills Moody 19
Chris Evert 18
Martina Navratilova 18

Most Grand Slam Doubles Titles

Men
John Newcombe 17
Todd Woodbridge 16

Women
Martina Navratilova 31
Pam Shriver 21

Most matches played at Wimbledon

Men: J.R. Borotra - 223 matches
Women: Martina Navratilova - 319 matches

Most Career Tournament Matches Won

Men
Jimmy Connors 1,222
Ivan Lendl 1,070
Guillermo Vilas 820

Women
Martina Navratilova 1,442
Chris Evert 1,304
Steffi Graf   900

Most Grand Slam Mixed Doubles Titles

Men
Frank Sedgman 8
Todd Woodbridge 7

Women
Margaret Smith Court 19
Billie Jean King 10

Longest 'Winning Streaks' in Modern Times

Men
Bjorn Borg   49 (1978)
Guillermo Vilas 46 (1977)
Ivan Lendl 44 (1981-82)

Women
Martina Navratilova, 74 (1984)
Steffi Graf, 66 (1989-90)
Navratilova, 58 (1986-87)

Youngest Winner of French Open

Men - Michael Chang (1989) 17 years and 3 months
Women - Monica Seles (1990) 16 years and 6 months

Most matches played at US Open

Men - Jimmy Connors – 115 matches (1970-89   1991-92)
Women - Chris Evert - 113   (1971-89)

Youngest and Oldest Australian Open Singles Champions

Youngest - Ken Rosewall (1953) 18 years, 2 months
Oldest-   Ken Rosewall (1972) 37 years, 2 months

Glossary

Ace A valid serve that the opposing player is unable to get their racket to and return.

Approach shot A shot used from inside the baseline to enable a player to attack the net.

Backspin Hitting the underside of the ball so that when it bounces, the ball brakes and bounces up.

Baseline The back line of the court which shows the court's length.

Cross-court shot A shot hit diagonally across the court rather than one hit straight over and down the line.

Double fault A point lost when the server fails to get either of their two serves in play.

Drop shot A delicate shot that barely clears the net and falls short in the opponent's court.

Match point A point which if won, results in one of the players or doubles teams winning the entire match.

Rally An exchange of shots between the players in a point.

Serve and volley A style of play that involves rushing toward the net immediately after the serve, in order to make a volley off the return.

Service break When one player wins a game while the other player is serving.

Service court The area on the other side of the net in which a serve must land in order to be legal.

Topspin Hitting over the top of the ball for to make it spin forward.

Volley Playing the ball in the air before it bounces.

Websites

www.atptennis.com
The homepage of the Men's professional tour, the ATP. This site is packed with features and biographies and results records of the leading players.

www.sonyericssonwtatour.com
The official internet site for the Women's professional tennis tour, the WTA. Here, you can read about news, competitions and player profiles.

www.lta.org.uk
The homepage of the Lawn Tennis Association, the organization that runs tennis in the UK. The website includes details of forthcoming competitions, spectator guides and profiles of top players.

www.tennisaustralia.com.au
The official body for tennis in Australia.

www.ontennis.com
A good general site for tennis containing the basic rules of the game, player and competition news and information on diet, technique and the game's history.

www.itftennis.com
The International Tennis Federation's website which contains information about tennis at all levels including news of future tournaments and coaching events.

OC11109.

Index

aces 8, 29
advantage 8
Agassi, Andrei 7
approach shot 18, 29

backhand drive 14–15
backhand grips 15
backhand lob 25
backhand smash 24
backhand volley 9, 17, 27
backspin 23, 25, 29
ball toss 20, 21
baselines 8, 29
Borotra, Jean 13, 28

centre mark 8, 9
chopper grip 21
courtcraft 18–19
courtesy 7, 11
courts 8, 26
cross-court shot 18, 29
Curran, Kevin 9

deuce 8
double fault 9, 29
doubles 26–7
drop shots 25, 29

faults 8–9, 20, 21
Federer, Roger 9, 19
foot fault 21
forehand drive 7, 12–13
forehand grip 13, 21
forehand volleys 16, 17

games 7
Graf, Steffi 7, 28
grand slam events 7
grips 13, 15, 21
ground strokes 12

Hepner, Jean 19

kit 11
knocking up 11

Laver, Rod 7, 28
line judges 7
lob shot 24–5
love 8

match point 29
matches 7
Mauresmo, Amelie 6
Murray, Andrew 17

Nadal, Rafael 9, 19
Navratilova, Martina 27, 28
Nelson, Vicky 19

one-handed backhand 14
one-handed backhand grip 15

Petrova, Nadia 27
players 6
practice 10
pros 7

rallies 19, 22, 26, 29
ready position 11, 12
receiving serve 22–3
records 28
rules 6, 7, 8–9

scoring 8, 9
serve and volley 29
service break 29
service court 8, 29
serving 8–9, 20–1, 22, 26
sets 7

shot down the line 18
slice 23, 25
smash shot 24
spin 23, 25, 29
Stosur, Samantha 6
stretching 10

teamwork 26
tiebreakers 7
topspin 23, 25, 29
two-handed backhand 15, 17

umpire 7

volleys 9, 16–17, 26, 27, 29

warming up 10
Williams, Serena 23, 24
Williams, Venus 23
Wimbledon 6, 7, 9, 13, 19, 27, 28

30